Poetry In The Spirit

Inspiration at your point of need…

By
JOHN L. GIVENS III

Xulon
PRESS

How to use this book

A poem-a-day may not keep the doctor away, however, thumb through these pages when you need a little encouragement and you are bound to find spiritual enrichment within the pages of this book.

Acknowledgments

I thank God that His grace, mercy, and peace is sufficient to supply all of our need. To all who participated in making this dream come true, may Almighty God richly bless you. A special thanks to my wife Ann for encouragement when I didn't believe myself that I would ever cross the finish line with the publication of this book. Thanks to Mother Emma Davis for her insights and encouragement.

Introduction

Poetry-In-The-Spirit is an inspired gift from God. It is my prayer that you will find a sea of inspiration and encouragement within the pages of this book.

The following scriptures kept me focused and encouraged during all stages of development and production of this book:

> Ecclesiastes 9:10   Whatsoever thy hand findeth to do, do it with thy might; for there is no work, nor device, nor knowledge, nor wisdom, in the grave, whither thou goest.
>
> 2 Timothy 1:7 For God hath not given us the spirit of fear; but of power, and of love, and of a sound mind.
>
> 2 Corinthians 5:7 (For we walk by faith, not by sight:)
>
> James 1:3,4 Knowing this, that the trying of your faith worketh patience. But let patience have her perfect work, that ye may be perfect and entire, wanting nothing.

This book is just a small indication of how God has revealed His sovereign providence in my life. May those who have an ear to hear, receive the fullness of God's engrafted Word. May your hearts, souls, and minds be consumed by His Spirit; that you may have life more abundantly.

Content

Creative Tangent

I took off on a creative tangent,
Not sure of where I was going.
Exploring the chambers of my imagination,
Contemplating without knowing.

I took off into the unknown,
Attempting to see what I could see.
Paralyzed by excitement,
The whole time asking, is this really happening to me?

These creative tangents are really neat,
Sometimes a great escape.
If I had a little more time,
Who knows what I could create!

The Fear of Failure

There is a fear of failure, so it seems,
This causes us not to live out our dreams.
Dreams, you just can't let them sit there,
Or they'll be like the clouds up in mid-air.

Floating adrift, as the winds blow,
Within your mind going to and fro'.
Beseech the Author of all mankind,
He'll bring peace unto your mind.
Explore the ideas of your heart,
Then ask God where you should start.

You will never grow bigger than your own thoughts,
If on your failures you become caught.
Fear sometimes plays tricks on you,
It will make you forget what you really can do.

"I can, I can!" a young lad did exclaim.
He said it so loud that fear forgot his name.
Believe in yourself and what you can do,
Then fear won't tap dance all over you.

In the will of God, man is capable of achieving the
impossible.

The Comforter

God is our pillow, on which we sleep,
He hears us when our spirits weep.
Go on, cry son and daughter too,
Because He will take care of you.

Life's journey is but a transient scheme,
On His sovereignty does hope gleam.

When troubles come, worry them not away,
But on your knees fall down and pray.
Just a little talk will make things right,
Then you won't be as up tight.

Walk in the spirit, and not in the flesh,
Then your soul will be greatly refreshed.
Peace will fall fresh upon you,
Make you so happy you won't know what to do.

Friends

As we travel life's courses friends float into view,
Sometimes many, sometimes few.
No major requirement between us two,
Just like me, and I'll like you.

Kids aren't real picky about their friends,
They're innocent and open, with no tied ends.
This seems acceptable at least for a short season,
Until they get "burned," without any reason.

Fellowship is good for ones soul,
And as we age it turns into gold.
Time has a way of seasoning us,
To grow in peace with much less fuss.

Seems like just yesterday, we grew up together,
Time drifted by, just like a feather.
The seasoning we've gained now etched in our faces,
Then came "good bye," we were off to the races.

So life goes on…and on…and on,
So life goes on.

I took a look at my children today;
My! I've come a long, long way.
The things I thought that I was, I'm not,
The things I thought that I wanted, I've got.

Share in this observation of friendship with me,
The value is priceless, so let's make a key.
The key must lock our friendship in place,
So that our love for each other won't get lost in the race.

Never Alone

I am not alone, because He's with me,
You may see me smile,
But, I'm not crazy.

When you experience the *peace* of the *Ancient of Days,*
You gain an understanding of His mysterious ways.

He walks with me and talks with me,
He creates my every stride,
Within this simple temple, the Holy Ghost abides.

Clouds

Floating through the eastern sky, lifted from the earth so high,
I asked myself the question, *why?*
Why did God do this for you and I?

Totally awesome the sight I see,
God was so gracious to make it for me.
Below the firmament there is human life, scuffling,
Struggling so full of strife.

Peace on earth, good will toward men,
Will God really ever do this again?
Only for the faithful…Only for the true…
Yes! Only for the committed few.

The clouds bring rain, sleet and snow,
Sometimes presenting themselves as our foe.
Woe, unto the man that curseth the rain,
For without it's substance there would be no grain.

God is sovereign, merciful and true.
He is too good to me and to you.
Blessed be *the Ancient of Days,* for His many mysterious ways.

They baffle us, they sting us, they shock our minds,
But the Creator made the clouds forever as a *shrine.*

The Missionary

I met some missionaries the other day,
They seemed to have so much to say.
They were a real family with teens,
I pondered what could I glean?

Following the letter of Jesus' commission,
They appeared to be on course with heaven's mission.
Looking for evidence of their love,
God's Spirit gave us a connection like a glove.

We prayed, we cried, we exchanged for a bit,
I thought is this my call? Does it fit?

Living For Now

Living for now can be a terrible thing,
No focus on tomorrow, can leave you in a sling.

There is a *Paradise* not very far away.
Are you waiting for another New Year's Day?
Resolutions grow short after one week,
They turn into lies and rarely reach their peak.

If we walk by faith and not by sight,
Then life in *Christ* can only be right.
This journey that we are on is only a conditioner,
And Jesus our Lord is the *Great Commissioner.*

Look at now with all it's lavish wealth,
And here comes tomorrow without any health.
What does "Now" do now?
Is it too late to ask God how?

Opportunity

Opportunity, like a feather in the wind,
You never know whether it will come back again.
If you miss it, don't you cry,
God, is the only one who really knows why.

Faith, a conglomeration of *somethingness,*
Suspended in the midst of *nothingness.*
Can I step-out?
Can I Try?
Or will I always look back and wonder *why?*

Opportunity, like a fruit on a tree,
When the stem is broken, is it really free?
Freedom, yes it's a funny thing,
On *opportunity* does it really cling?

So, you want to have it your way?
Will *opportunity* present itself today?
Trust the *Lord* in everything you do,
So *opportunity* does not slip past you…

What You Have Chosen

What you have chosen, is a serious thing,
Life, the endeavor to which men do cling.
"Choose you this day whom you will serve!"
The Lord He will guide you and not let you curve.

Choice is a freedom we all exercise;
To be lost in sin or to be circumcised

Joshua spoke boldly in that fifteenth verse,
The words he exclaimed, he did not rehearse.

Serve the Lord in *sincerity* and in *truth,*
Should you limit your allegiance, you will live in a booth.
Going to and fro' in a precarious way,
Wondering whom it will be, you will serve today.

"As for me and my house, we will serve the Lord!"
For He requires *commitment* and this He rewards.

Death

Death, seems so severe,
Especially to those who are very near.

Death, has been conquered by Christ,
Nevertheless, from His words we won't take advice.

Should you get lost within the trap of time,
Remember that *The Omega* ended death's chime…

Rapture

I had a dream this morning that the Lord came back. It was so real to me. I can't recall everything that took place, but I do remember the chaos that was going on during the revelation of His return to the earth. I remember people scattering as if a bunch of ants that just had their domain destroyed by a **giant human**. The fact of the matter is, this is the way He shall return…"Like a theft in the night."

> Matthew 25:13
> "Watch therefore, for ye know neither the day nor the hour wherein the Son of man cometh."

GOD:
Good Ole Dad

Good Ole Dad is still the same,
Holy and omnipotent, He'll never change.
Even as a snake sheds its skin,
From our backs He stripes the sin.

Oh, how awesome is the King of all Kings,
From everlasting to everlasting He encompasses everything.

Yes, Even from Genesis to Revelations,
His Kingdom is above all other nations.
God my friend and my peace keeper.
The Ancient of Days, even my souls' great reaper.
The harvest is ripe, but the laborers are few,
Until His kingdom comes on earth He'll forever be true.

Provocative Proclamation

He spoke in the cloak of parables,
To those without the truth, it was unbearable.

Lost souls He did seek,
The uncompromised truth did He speak.

When He opened His mouth He did reveal,
The secrets of the world, with great, great zeal.

"Hypocrites! Hypocrites!" He did exclaim,
To the false prophets who knew not His name.

A deposit of equity, on earth He did pause,
Notwithstanding, He was hated without cause.

Jealousy

Jealousy, can rip you all apart,
It can even pierce your heart.

Jealousy, can cause your nerves to tie,
It can even make you weep and cry.

When jealousy gets the best of you,
This is what you've got to do.

Beseech the Lord in a humble way,
Very fervently begin to *pray!*

My Father, who maketh a way
Help me, calm me, please *this day!*
Make mine eyes to see clear again,
Set me in the starting blocks to begin.
Make me to run in the righteous path,
Cleanse me, wash me, give me a bath.

Love in spite, we are admonished to do,
Because oh God, it pleases you.
Perfection; yes, only if we try,
Then jealousy would have no heart…
No heart to pry…

Partners

Husbands and wives carry a very heavy load,
Two people submissive in their place of adobe.
Very strange, this union we commit to,
Drawing nigh into one, but this is not new.

Communication is the element that helps us to know,
Love is the ingredient that makes us grow.

The revelations of life give us an edge,
Around our frames they are a protective hedge.
They provide us guidance in a sometimes painful way,
So...*restrained* we can always stay.

The Wall

Up against the wall and I can't stop now,
Aliens observe and wonder how?
So committed, so determined is this soul,
How in the world can he be so bold?

Swiftly and diligently he travels life's way,
Aware that he's a foreigner, not here to stay.
If the wall has got you down, just look up!
Let Jesus into your heart and with Him you'll sup'.

Fix your mind on the positive,
Let God be your guide,
Never let Satan change your stride.

The race is not given to the swift or to the strong,
And with God as your Coach, you can never go wrong.
If the wall has got you down, just look up!
Because God is the one who will fill your cup.

A Step of Faith

If I step out on faith,
What's the worst that can happen?
If I run the good race,
How far can I go?

If I walk in the narrow path,
How tight will it be?
If I cry unto the Lord,
Will I be made free?

If I reach for higher heights,
How high will I go?
If I go where I have not gone,
Who will I know?

If I sing my psalms of praise,
Will I be the only one in tune?
If I clap my hands for joy,
Will this be proper in June?

Too Far to Escape

I'm sitting in the midst of my despair,
No one here to give a care.
My heart's arrested by an itch that burns,
My body's too numb to even turn.

My weakness says, Hey let's pray.
My sorrow says, Hey no way!
To sing a song may even be right,
But, my psychology is so up-tight.

Loose me from this yoke I pray.
There has got to be some easier way?
Childhood seems an easy escape,
But, reality will not rend its cape.

Reality is the world to live in,
No more fantasy, to enhance my sin.
Where am I going and what shall I do?
Please, speak to me Son of God,
Now I can listen to You.

Men

Do we know *who* we are?
Do we know *whose* we are?

God made us strong in a very special clay,
He made us first, to lead the way,
Then gave He us woman, to help us through the day,
Give us stability so we would not sway.

Men, so dominant, so very shrewd,
Ignorance, the deterrent that makes us so rude.

Adam gave names to all cattle and beast.
That was no small task, to say the least.
What are we doing to help mankind?
Or do we just sit back and recline?

Now, is the time to take our post.
Men, get-up and become the host!

Turn-a-loose of the form and fashion,
Let's attack this world with a mad passion.
Present yourself for *righteousness sake,*
So that no one can ever call you a *fake.*

Bless the Lord for seeing you through,
For heaven's feast table this we do.

The Man That I Am

As a maturing man I am often challenged by my past.
A past that I did not live, but I can not escape.
The distress of bondage creeps up on me as I look into the
faces of other men that look like me.
Men who appear to be encumbered by the mental shackles
that keeps us bound.

That bondage is an unrelenting mind set,
Whose principal agents are *fear*, *ignorance*, and *laziness*.
Fear, because it causes us not to live out our righteous
dreams.
Ignorance, because we tend to cling to the vanity of our
minds.
Laziness, because we are not developing the endurance to
try a new.

Who is at fault?
Who else really cares?
Is there anyone who sees this like me?
Can I really make a difference?
Is it really worth it?

The mental gymnastics that I participate in wears me out!
Trying to maintain the proper perspective, faced with
tremendous odds.
Who am I to make a difference in a world that sometimes
seems to hate me?
Am I dreaming the impossible dream?

I have a will to try that comes from above.
The transforming grace from God strengthens my go.
The knowledge of His mystery gives me boldness.
My understanding of His power affords my courage.

Without a positive image of myself it's tough to rise above
it all.
Let me see myself as a victorious champion who *must*
endure hardness.
Who *must* overcome!
Then maybe I have a fighting chance.
Maybe then, I can be the man that I am.

From the Outside In

From the outside in,
I stand bold and tall.
From the inside out,
I stumble and fall.

From the outside in,
I shine like the sun.
From the inside out,
I'm like a loaded gun.

From the outside in,
My character looks set.
From the inside out,
I gamble and bet.

From the outside in,
I appear to find my way.
From the inside out,
I go so far astray.

You see me from the outside in,
God hears me from the inside out,
He knows my frailties and comforts me with His Holy Spirit.

Walking Post

I know that God can supply all my need,
Even start a flower from a seed.

I know that He sits up on high,
And even lights up the sky.

Jesus came from Galilee,
To save a wretch like you…like me.
Oh, Lord I thank You so!

"Thank you," seems not enough,
For the abundance that You have given us,
But Father I do thank You!

When I hear the ocean's great loud roars,
And I see the waves halting at the shores,
I am reminded of the power of Your Might.

When my finite mind,
Contemplates the creation of all mankind,
Oh, how I take Your ***gifts of grace*** for granted,
They seem so sure!

When I think on Your ***infinity***,
Which initiated all eternity,
How great Thou art!

You told me to ***owe no one,***
Except that which cannot be bought with funds.

Love, so beautiful and pure,
So sweet I could never, ever endure.
But true love can only come from You,
As does the early morning dew.

Father, please lead me 'til I die,
Oh, hear my yearning cry.
To be Your servant is my greatest desire,
Enlighten my sole, my heart *inspire!*

Strong Enough

I want to be strong enough to love my neighbor as myself,
Strong enough to rest in the power of God's might.
I want to be strong enough to reach with my last ounce of
courage,
Strong enough even, to fight the good fight.

I want to be strong enough to be a friend that will listen,
Strong enough to listen with concern,
Concerned enough to comfort my dear loved ones,
Even when they have experienced a bad turn.

I want to be strong enough to make it through the good
times.
I want to be strong enough to take it through the bad.
I want to be strong enough to carry my own burdens.
Strong enough even, to carry when I'm sad.

My strength in its weakness is strong,
Because by faith I go on.
I am called from darkness unto light,
For my eternal home, one day I'll take flight.

I want to be strong enough to loose when I have to.
I want to be strong enough to win in God's grace.
I want to be strong enough to let go when it's not mine to
hold tight.
Strong enough even to trust 'til my faith turns to sight.

My Friend Jesus

When I find myself in a query of thought about why I sometimes feel the way that I do; not necessarily good and not necessarily bad. Especially after a loved one may have been insensitive to me and over looked my external emotions without a care. It is then that I am reminded to run to my friend Jesus for comfort, encouragement, and understanding. He is my helper when no one else has time to listen to my thoughts, so I spend a lot of time with Him, because it seems quite often that I am misunderstood. I heard how King David in the Old Testament, encouraged himself in the Lord. I now understand that to a greater degree, because I have had many times when I needed to be encouraged, but no one was around to do the job.

Maybe you have had times like this when you just needed someone to talk to, someone who would hear your cares and concerns, but not let the whole world know about them. Someone that you could trust with the secretes of your heart and the treasures of your hopes. I recommend Jesus Christ to you. He is a friend of mine. He not only hears me, but He responds to me with peace and joy in the midst of my sorrows, pains, and doubts. He sustains me in situations that others tend to fall apart in. My relationship with Him is so sure from His perspective that I do not have to concern myself with Him changing under pressure. If anything I have to concern myself with my changing towards Him under the pressures of life.

Yes, I recommend Jesus to you, because without Him I do not know where I would be right now. Possibly strung out on drugs trying to self medicate. Possibly lost in an alcoholic's bottle trying to drink my troubles away. Possibly locked up in prison, because I acted-out inappropriately when someone stepped on my toes or did not fit into the ideals of my wants and wishes. I am sure that it has been Jesus in my life that has made the difference.

Please if not for me, for yourself find out who Jesus Christ really is. The best thing that can happen is He will become your friend too.

Notes

Notes

Notes

Notes

CPSIA information can be obtained at www.ICGtesting.com
Printed in the USA
BVOW07s0923080714

358462BV00001B/20/P

9 781624 190117